LIVE LIKE A
L.Y.O.N
LIFT YOURSELF OVER NEGATIVITY

POETRY SPELLBOOK SERIES

VOL 1
SPELLS OF COURAGE

A SELECTION OF SPELLS:
POEMS, PROSE, PHOTOS, & PROMPTS

ELEVATE YOUR MIND
EMPOWER YOUR LIFE

CREATED & CAST BY:
ELLE DE LYON

LIVE LIKE A L.Y.O.N: POETRY SPELLBOOK

First Edition 2025

Library and Archives Canada Cataloguing in Publication
Elle de Lyon
Live Like a L.Y.O.N.: Lift Yourself Over Negativity / Elle de Lyon.
ISBN 978-1-998245-56-7 (paperback)
ISBN 978-1-998245-57-4 (hardcover)
1. Self-help poetry. 2. Personal development—Poetry. 3. Emotional healing. I. Title.

Cover Art by Elle de Lyon
Illustrations and Photography by Elle de Lyon
Audio Production by PDA Global Media
Published in Canada by Eva-Michelle & Family Publishing
www.evamichelleandfamily.com

Printed on Turtle Island

TO LEARN MORE:

www.iamelledelyon.com

CONTENTS

——————✦——————

FOREWORD

---·+·---

In the following pages, you will be introduced to a new voice with a unique perspective on how each of us must confront and come to terms with an ubiquitous aspect of the human condition: the nebulous noise of negativity that can sometimes restrain and restrict our personal growth.

Through her poetry, elle de Lyon is able to share with us her personal journey to overcoming negativity and developing a growth mindset of power, purpose and mental/spiritual prosperity.

She provides us with a series of prescriptions that we can use in our self-healing activities, and ultimately, in our attempt to live like a L.Y.O.N ---Lifting Yourself Over Negativity.

Bravo! Bravo! Bravo!

-THE AUTHOR'S FADA
P.M.A DE LYON

DEDICATION & ACKNOWLEDGEMENTS

———————✦———————

This book is for the ones who came before me,
and the ones coming after—
for my inner child
And my niece and nephews
you are my why
The reason I break curses
rewrite stories
and pour light into shadow
so you can know a deeper freedom
to live your legacy
as our ancestors wildest dreams

To my parents—thank you for your sacrifices and support
You crossed continents so I could live where possibility exists.
You taught me to turn struggle into strength.
That alchemy lives in me now.

To my sisters—
your love, wisdom, and presence shaped me.
I carry us all in these pages.

To the ones who started this journey and remain only in spirit
"Fam, I am doing everything we talked about."
To JV who illuminated the path on my sustainable creative journey.
To Elijah for your insight,
Your light lives on in these pages.

To my mentors—Coco, Carlos, D'bi, Lorraine—
thank you for encouraging me to birth my vision through this book
To Anastasia, Shadel TBG, Cat, Adrian, Jajè, Kabrena—
thank you for witnessing the seed of these pages before they
bloomed into these chapters and all of your support and feedback.

To the community spaces and stages that nurtured my voice—
R.I.S.E. Edutainment, Blk Men Style, Blk Book Fair, Unity Charity,
Our Crib Uncut, Lvl Up Media, Nia Centre, Afiwi Groove,
Madewell Productions, PDA Global Media, Sandbox Studios,
Sound Bites, Black Physicians of Tomorrow, Live it Wear it,
Institute of Cultural Affairs Canada, Yinnergy, Stay Relevant,
Adornment Stories, For The Writers Circle, Beat Cave,
The Hook & Co., Fill the Blnk, Content Day, Sunset Cypher,
Street Voices, Leverage Lens, Lorraine Lawson Vocal Studio,
City Leaders Program, CEE Toronto, Tropicana Community
Services, MACCUP, YRAACC, Institute , Loud Army, Toronto 2.0,
Kujipenda, TAIBU, Right Beside You, Rudy Ray Band
—thank you for pouring into me.

To every organization that gave me
a mic, a moment, or a platform—
I have been honoured to serve and be shaped by the work.

To my creative production family: Randell, Jason, Kajaea, Abby,
Alliston, Mohamed, Pria, Ditto, Igor, Val, Andre, Sanaaj, Wiz, Tony,
Mark, Janice it is an honour to make magic with you.

To the dreamers—
those who dare to believe in themselves
in a world designed to diminish—
this is for you.

This book is how I honour those
who are no longer with us—
ancestors known and unknown,
and every soul I have loved
and lost along the way.

To the ones I was inspired not to be
you handed me boxes of darkness,
and it took time,
but I finally understood:
this too was a gift.
To those who hurt me—
and to the one's that I hurt in return.

vi

Thank you for the mirrors, the shadows, the echoes.
You showed me the edges of myself,
so I could choose to soften them,
sharpen them, or set them free.

Sometimes the echoes linger, and we become the bully in our own mind—repeating their lies in our own voice, until the wounds wear our name.

It took time to realize that voice wasn't mine alone. There was someone inside me—fierce, protective, and loud—trying to keep me safe the only way she knew how. I named her LYON. She's sharp-tongued, raw, and relentless. But she's loyal. I honour her not by silencing her, but by listening with compassion. By choosing to rise above what hurt us. By remembering we are more than survival—we are transformation.

I dedicate these pages to my inner child, and to every version of me—who I was, who I am, and who I am still becoming. I honour them all with love.

To those who resonate with these spells, thank you—for your audacity to hope, your courage to evolve, and your will to live like a L.Y.O.N: Lifting Yourself Over Negativity.

Lift yourself over the naysayers—the No's, Never's, and Not's.
Lift yourself over every label, every cage, every "you'll never" whispered behind your back.

May your roar rewrite the rules.
May your rise make silence loud.
And may you wear the crown you forged from every "not enough" you once believed.

You are the spell. You are the proof.
The end of one chapter is the beginning of the next.

AUTHORS NOTE

———— ✦ ————

They said I was cursed. I know now I was called.

I was born carrying what some might label as curses:
 A chronic illness.
 A mind they could not control.
 A name they refused to pronounce.

But I've come to understand this—curses, when transmuted, become gifts.

Each so-called curse held a lesson. Each challenge, a mirror.

What once felt like a burden became a bridge. What once silenced me now strengthens my voice. I found my purpose in the pain. And I've learned: problems are not punishments—they're possibilities. Through it all, I discovered that the very things meant to break me became the blueprint for my becoming.

The 1st Transmutation --The Gift of the Body

I was born with a chronic condition—an invisible affliction—where my immune system misfired, attacking what it was meant to protect. From birth to age three, I couldn't play outside or attend daycare like other children. My body couldn't withstand the environments others moved through with ease. So I stayed inside. Stayed still. Stayed silent. Not by choice—but by necessity.

And yet, in that stillness, something sacred stirred. Before I had words to name it, I discovered spelling, writing, thinking, and mindfulness—practices that would become my lifelines. Each flare-up was a signal, a call to explore and engage more deeply with my well-being. I learned to listen, to honor the messages my body sent, and to respond with care.

My body didn't just hold me; it spoke to me—through continuous flare-ups that came in waves. Sometimes familiar, sometimes brand new. Allergies developed to things I had once tolerated. Sensitivities faded to things I was once allergic to.

Each shift was unpredictable, each reaction a new message.

Doctors gave me medications to suppress these flare-ups, to quiet the symptoms. And while these medicines helped in some ways, they also harmed me in others—masking pain without addressing root causes, creating new challenges even as they eased old ones.

I continue to learn that the medical standards I've been held to were built on colonial frameworks—standards that often ignore the full humanity of those they serve.

True healing demands more than treatment; it demands decolonization.

It demands reclaiming joy and wholeness beyond systems that don't always see us.

My body became both a refuge and a challenge—the space where struggle met strength. It taught me patience in the pause, power in presence, and grace in the grind.

In that journey, I realized: strength doesn't always roar. Survival is a sacred song. Healing moves in circles, not lines.

This was the first transmutation.

What others called a curse, I now call a gift.

The body that broke me open also built me whole.

The Second Transmutation - A Mind They Couldn't Control

I was three years old when the classroom first became a cage—a place where curiosity was a crime and brilliance was boxed in silence. Every time I raised my hand, reaching for recognition, I was told to lower it, to quiet my questions, to dim my desire. I had answers aplenty—straight A's in academics, yet straight N's in the notes about me: Needs Improvement, Not Listening, Not Quiet Enough. I excelled on paper, aced every test, yet my spirit was suppressed. Instead of encouragement, I got containment. Instead of acceleration, I got accusation.

They never asked, "Where do we place this plentiful brilliance?" They just wanted me to stop shining, stop stirring, stop standing out. It was as if my mind—too bright, too bold—exposed what they lacked inside themselves. So they sent me to the back of the classroom, then out the door. When I wasn't in the nurse's office for my body, I was in the principal's office for my behavior.

A record grew—a roster of recesses lost, removals recorded, notes sent home. That record became the reason I was denied entry into the gifted program—the one place where I could have soared. They put me in behavioral—same work, different label. One label for the brilliant, one for the broken. And they decided I was broken.

But the truth is—the system never changed. It never shifted, never softened, never saw me for who I truly was. But I did. Standing out—not in spite of, but because of—became my superpower. I outstood my circumstances. Outshone the limits they tried to place on me. Outlived their doubts and definitions. Nothing changed about the system. But I changed what I believed it was meant to do for me. I decided to define standing out as practice designed for becoming outstanding.

Suppression of expression leads to depression.

I went into high school carrying the weight of the label they gave me—believing I was bad. I even named myself badgirl15, wearing it like armor. Suspended more times than I can count, my grades started to slip—not from lack of ability, but because I believed the worst about myself. My focus scattered, and I poured myself into chaos—talking tough, acting unbothered while holding everything inside.

But outside school—in my community—I felt something different. I felt seen. Connected. Capable. Then she appeared—a Black female guidance counsellor who shared my cultural background. The first adult in school who truly saw me beyond my behavior and record. We'd just begun working together when I got into a physical fight— my first and only—and was banned from school property, missing my graduation. Still, her presence planted a seed. Even as I left that system, I began to seek something new: real support, real purpose, and a path beyond the labels: Community. Programs. Possibility.

My mom stood by me—as she always had—even as I walked away from that school. The mentor who first truly saw me stayed connected, a family friend. Together, they found ways to engage me in community and support my growth. They knew that healing and belonging go beyond the classroom walls.

When the school system gave up on me, my mom didn't. She enrolled me in a Guyanese Canadian cultural pageant that changed my life. It wasn't just about beauty—it was about finding my voice, presence, and purpose. As the youngest contestant, I spoke about the power of mentorship—being guided, not graded. I was crowned runner-up and won a trip home to Guyana for my family. That moment reshaped how I saw myself and what was possible.

It was the start of rewriting my story, stepping into my power, and building the community I—and many others—needed: to be seen, not sorted. In that moment, I wasn't bad. I was bold. Becoming. Victorious.

More than the crown or the trip, I reconnected with my roots—my legacy, my lineage. I began to live fiercely and with purpose, chasing a dream to break the generational curses that held people like me back from reaching their full potential.

I reframed what they once called wild and unruly as rebellion with a cause. That cause became creating inclusive, diverse, and equitable spaces led by those who reflect the cultures and communities they serve. In serving my community, I found something sacred: reflection, restoration, reciprocity. I wasn't too much—I was the mirror, memory, and momentum of those who came before me. Never meant to be contained. Meant to channel, to challenge, to change.

This was my second transmutation.
What they once called a broken mind
was a mind too brilliant to be boxed in—
too luminous for their limits.

The Third Transmutation - A Name They Refused to Pronounce

My last name is de Lyon, pronounced Duh – Lee – Yon. My parents came to the school and explained it clearly, but they didn't want to say it right. They wanted to say it their way. So they called me "the lion" — like an animal, something to fear, something to tame. They butchered my name, laughed at it, passed it around like a joke, and taught others to do the same.

It's a French name, yes, but we're not French. We are Guyanese — descendants of people colonized by the French. Even my name is complicated, compromised, not one my ancestors chose, but one I tried to wear with pride. Still, they wouldn't let me. They turned my name into a symbol of aggression.

My first-grade teacher told me, "You might be 'the lion,' but you're not the king of this classroom. Save it for the jungle." That line didn't stay in the classroom — it followed me everywhere.

It followed me into the streets, where I joined a gang not out of choice but because the system had boxed me in. The label of "bad" was heavy, and I wore it like armor. It followed me into hospitals where nurses mispronounced my name like a taunt and likened my calls for advocacy to a lion's roar — something fierce, something to be feared.

Last year, I had a flare-up, one that could have been managed, but was mismanaged because of the color of my skin. They called me "ferocious" and told me I wouldn't be helped. Even with diagnosis in hand, they said my options were limited — limited by budget lines, not by my needs.

I spent months in hospitals, test after test, held to a standard that ignored me. Even when their own data showed treatments failing, they refused to offer alternatives — until I nearly died. Not metaphorically — literally. I was placed on life support, not because my body failed, but because the system did. A system that could not see the fullness of my body, my mind, or my story. A system that wanted me to be silent and standard. But I am neither.

This wasn't the first time institutions misdiagnosed me. In school, I passed their gifted tests only for them to redraw the finish line. I surpassed their expectations, and they responded with suppression. They renamed my brilliance a behavioral issue. My questions became "defiance." Suppression led to depression. And from that, I discovered the power of expression — and even deeper than that, the gift of perception. Perception changed everything. It allowed me to see beyond the walls they built. It reminded me the problem was never me — it was the box they kept trying to fit me in.

Writing became the key. I wrote letters, emails, proposals, applications. My writing opened doors that had been locked for years. It gave me the power to advocate for myself when no one else would. For a long time, writing was my refuge—a place where I could move unseen, speak freely, and rise above the silencing of my reputation, race, and body.

I used to fear being misunderstood. Not anymore. Now, every time fear tries to hold me back, I write. What once felt like a dead end becomes a blueprint. What once felt like defeat becomes testimony.

People always ask me how I got to be where I am. Honestly, it feels like I've skipped over a lot of the hard stuff—like a movie cutting straight to the highlights. But there was so much that happened between graduating high school and going to university. That's when the real work began. I was forced to confront parts of myself and the world that school never prepared me for. The lessons I learned about standing out finally started to make sense. Through mentorship—something I had to seek out for myself—I learned how to stand out in ways that felt empowering, not isolating. I learned that courage isn't something you're born with; it's something you build by facing what you're afraid of, again and again.

The truth is, the person you see today isn't who I've always been. Writing helped me get here. I've always been a thinker—someone whose thoughts came in the form of words. Writing gave those thoughts direction. That's when I began to realize that words are spells. What you think, say, and write has power. And when I started casting those spells intentionally—on paper, in doctor's offices, in boardrooms, on stages—everything began to shift. When I went away to university, I stepped outside of familiar cultural norms and finally leaned into talk therapy, even though it was taboo in my community. It changed my life—and my family's—breaking generational cycles and opening new doors. Around that same time, my chronic illness returned. Traditional medicine didn't work, so I sought out alternative healing. The five practices that now ground me—breathwork, meditation, mindful movement, nourishment, and mindful thinking—taught me how to live with intention. Mindful thinking, for me, means writing things down, talking things through, reflecting so I can respond—rather than react—to a world that hasn't always made space for me. Writing helped me take up space.

This Book Is One of Those Spaces

More than a collection of poems, spells, and stories, this book offers a sacred, intentional framework for transformation. Within these pages, you'll find the core elements guiding your journey: the Equation, a mindset-shifting formula; the Elevated Principle, a value to align your intentions; the Adinkra Symbol, ancestral wisdom from West African symbology; the Chakra Centre, energetic grounding through ancient systems; the Spell Type— your method of transformation; the Spell Theme—the emotional focus; and the Spell Affirmation, a powerful "I AM" to rewire your inner dialogue and activate your elevated self.

Each book in the L-Y-O-N series follows this framework, designed to help you Lift Yourself Over Negativity and walk the path of self-mastery. These books are interactive tools to help you uncover pride and live like a LYON. We begin with Spells of Courage—the root of all elevation. This book is your foundation, like the Root Chakra: your base, your anchor. It calls you to prepare—for battles within and beyond. Just as the Akoben, the Akan war horn, signals readiness, this book awakens your inner warrior.

Words are spells—they can limit or liberate, elevate or oppress. They shape how we move through the world and through ourselves. These are Spells of Courage because it takes courage to explore, engage, and choose freedom when born into a cage. This book speaks to the child who didn't know better and the adult shaped by wounds. Forgiveness and liberation live here.

You can experience this book in three sacred dimensions: through voice (spoken word), visuals (videos and imagery), and verse (music). This work isn't just read—it's felt, seen, heard, and lived.

Elevate your mindset. Empower your life —This call pulses through every page, spell, and poem.

The L-Y-O-N series spans nine books. By the ninth, it will carry the voices of all who have joined this journey—each inspiring the next, creating a growing community. By 2029, hundreds of thousands of LYONs will lift themselves and others over negativity, living with pride and purpose, reshaping the world.

At the close of each book, you're invited to write back—to me, to yourself, to your inner child, and to the adult still learning to roar. This ongoing dialogue—your reflections and reclamation—is part of the spell. Through it, pain becomes possibility, and your story is reborn.

Wherever I go—healthcare, education, community—I bring art as my agency. I use it to shift narratives, challenge oppression, and demand representation. I am decolonizing with words, which I see as art—an act of defiance, a tool of remembrance, and a pathway to freedom. Art transforms the spaces that once tried to contain me.

The systems may not change overnight, but when we shift how we see them—and how we see ourselves—we change everything. Whatever you face, let it ignite a fire within. Make it mean something only you can define.

This is more than an author's note. It's a call to action. An invitation. A vow: To reframe your story. To reclaim your glory. And to live like a LYON --Lifting Yourself Over Negativity.

The roar begins here—and the journey continues in you.

With power in the pen, and purpose in every page—

Words are spells; Cast carefully,

Elle de Lyon

L.Y.O.N. POETRY BOOK SERIES OVERVIEW

A 9-Part Collector's Series for Self-Mastery Through Poetry, Practice & Power

The L.Y.O.N. Poetry Book Series is a soul-centered collection for those ready to elevate by lifting themselves over life's most common forms of negativity. Designed as both a poetic journey and a toolkit for emotional mastery, this 9-part collector's series guides readers through the process of healing and empowerment, one emotion at a time.

Each book centers on a core emotional challenge and includes foundational elements like spell themes—emotional energies such as Courage, Peace, and Intention—alongside mindset equations that transform pain into purpose. Readers will also discover elevated principles that strengthen resilience, Adinkra symbols representing West African ancestral wisdom, chakra alignments derived from Asia for energetic balance, and various spell types, including incantations, affirmations, and mantras. Every volume functions as a ritual, blending poetry, reflection, and mindfulness to help readers transmute trauma, clarify their purpose, and embody personal power.

But why nine books? The number 9 holds profound significance across spiritual and mathematical traditions. In numerology, it symbolizes completion, mastery, healing, and wisdom—making it the ideal number for a transformation series. In sacred geometry, the 9-pointed enneagram represents unity and the soul's journey toward wholeness. Even mathematically, every multiple of 9 reduces back to 9, reinforcing the idea that everything returns to its essence. This series is that essence—where power, purpose, and poetry converge.

For me, the number 9 holds deep personal power. I was born in the 9th month, on the 29th day—9, 2, 9. A palindrome. A number that reads the same forward and backward. It reminds me that healing isn't linear—it loops, revisits, and returns. This symmetry anchors me to the energy of 9: endings that lead to renewal, and mastery earned through cycles of transformation.

That's why this series is made up of 9 books. The first 8 guide you through core lessons—truths I had to learn and unlearn. The 9th is your spellbook: the space where you complete your journey and claim your own power. It's not an ending. It's your return to self.

Collecting the L.Y.O.N. Series Means:
A complete map to emotional and spiritual mastery
Engagement with ancestral and modern healing practices
The power to reframe your story and reclaim your glory

This is more than poetry.

It's your journey, your elevation, your spellwork.

Let each book be your guide—and Book 9 be your liberation, your return, your roar.

L.Y.O.N POETRY SPELLBOOK SERIES
ELEMENTS

BOOK	SPELL THEME	EQUATION
1	Spells of Courage	Fear − Doubt = Courage
2	Spells of clarity	Silence + Awareness = Clarity
3	Spells of growth	Pain × Love) ÷ Time = Growth
4	Spells of liberation	Courage + Clarity = Liberation
5	Spells of integrity	Liberation + Integrity = Aligned Action
6	Spells of intention	Liberation × Reflection + Intention = Transformation
7	Spells of peace	Intention + Rhythm = Inner Peace
8	Spells of Abundance	Peace × Love + Gratitude = Abundance

L.Y.O.N POETRY SPELLBOOK SERIES
ELEMENTS CONT'D

PRINCIPLE	ADINKRA SYMBOL	
EXPLORE & ENGAGE	AKOBEN	
LISTENING & LEARNING	SANKOFA	
EMBODY & EXPRESS	NKYIMKYIM	
VISION & VALUE	FAWOHODIE	
ALIGN & APPLY	DUAFE	
TRANSMUTE & TRANSFORM	MATE MASIE	
EMPOWER & EVOLVE	DONO	
DECIDE, DEFINE, DESIGN, DEVOTE	ADINKRAHENE	

THE L.Y.O.N POETRY SPELLBOOK STRUCTURE

---+.+---

Core Elements Included in Every Volume

Each book in the L-Y-O-N series follows an intentional framework designed to help you Lift Yourself Over Negativity and walk the path of self-mastery.

Every spellbook includes the following elements:

The Equation
A mindset-shifting formula that unlocks the intention behind the spell and offers a lens for transformation.

The Elevated Principle
A guiding value or approach that supports emotional and spiritual alignment.

The Adinkra Symbol
A traditional West African symbol that carries ancestral wisdom and represents the theme of the spell.

Chakra Centre
An energetic focal point drawn from ancient traditions from Asia, connecting the spell's theme to your body and spirit.

Spell Type
The form of transformation the spell offers—i.e. Transmutation, Conjuring, Chanting, Casting, or Envisioning.

Spell Theme
The central emotional and energetic focus of the spell.

Spell Affirmation

Affirmations in this book are intentional spells—each "I AM" redefines your inner dialogue and activates your elevated self. Rooted in the truth that what follows "I AM" defines you, they help reprogram limiting beliefs into empowered ones.

What's Included

Each spell features:
- Poetry Spells for reflection and activation
- Guided Journal Prompts for exploration
- Embodiment Practices for integration
- Interactive Pages for co-creation and self-expression
- Soundscapes and soundtracks to experience the spells in different mediums

The Intention

These spellbooks are both sacred tools and interactive journeys. They help you uncover the pride within and live like a LYON: Lifting Yourself Over Negativity.

ABOUT THIS SPELL — VOL. I, BOOK I
GROUNDING IN POWER TO RISE THROUGH FEAR

———————— ✛ ————————

We begin with Spells of Courage — the root of all elevation.

This first spellbook activates your foundation, much like the root chakra. It is a call to prepare — for the battles within and the ones we face in the world. Just as the Akoben, the war horn of the Akan people, sounds the call to readiness, this book awakens your inner warrior.

You are invited to begin the essential work of grounding yourself, facing your fears, and taking action from a place of self-trust. Courage isn't the absence of fear — it's the decision to move through it. This book supports you in exploring your inner landscape and staying engaged, even when life feels overwhelming.

Equation
Fear – Doubt = Courage

Elevated Principle
Explore & Engage

Adinkra Symbol
Akoben — The War Horn (Twi, Akan)
A call to readiness and action. Akoben reminds us that courage begins with the willingness to respond.

Chakra Centre
Root Chakra (Muladhara, Sanskrit)
The root represents our base, our anchor, and our sense of safety. To stand strong in the face of fear, we must feel the ground beneath our feet.

Spell Type
Transmutation — Turn fear into fuel.

Spell Theme
Courage

Spell Affirmation
I AM exploring my fear and engaging my power.

Each poem, prompt, and practice in this spellbook moves you one step forward—guiding you to lift yourself over negativity by walking through it with courage and purpose.

This is your starting point.
Your foundation.
Your first spell.

This is more than a poetry book.

It's a spellbook for self-mastery.

A cycle of transformation using the ancient powers of transmutation, alchemy, conjuring, chanting, casting, and envisioning—practices that remind us that words are spells.

The poems, lyrics, and prose in this book were intentionally crafted as spells you can cast on yourself— tools to summon courage, clarity, growth, liberation, integrity, intention, peace, and abundance. They were written to help you elevate your mindset, shift your energy, and empower your life.

Because each word—written or spoken—carries its own vibration and magic.

And the way you speak to yourself?

That's where transformation begins.

Words are spells.
Cast them Carefully.

Live like a

L.Y.O.N.
Lift Yourself Over Negativity

Stay Elevated

✦ SPELL 1 ✦

SPELLS OF COURAGE

TRANSMUTING FEAR INTO FUEL

The following pages hold the words I wrote when I needed to transform fear into fuel. Through this process, I began to transmute trauma into testimony and turn barriers into building blocks.

These are my raw, honest reflections — offering you a glimpse of the power in reclaiming your voice and owning your healing.

Walk your path with courage, on purpose — meaning you are on assignment, fully showing up for your own transformation.

LIFT YOURSELF OVER N.....
THE NEW 'N" WORD

I am **nirvana** in motion, a super**nova novel**,
Namaste to the past — I am a **numinous** gospel,
Navigating new narratives, negating negativity.
Endowing **new** worlds, **new** waves, **new** realms, **new** reigns
in divinity, I am **never** ending I am in**finity**
Not your **niche** —
I'm the **nexus**, where the codes cross and connect us.
You boxed in — I break out, flexin'.
The system bends when I bless it.
Never the token — I am the template.
Rooted in ruins but rewriting with reverence.
Not a guest here — I am the genesis.
They gatekeep, I generate entrances.

You **nod numb**, I **narrate newness, never** mimicking
I am the muse made to move this.
Neutral noses notice fury as flair —
I flip, finesse, fill and flood the air.
I'm **not** your type — I'm the turning table,
the **net** you can't **nab** or disable.

They **named** me wrong, but I re**named** the block,
Now every wall speaks my **name**, and every corner talks.
They **named** me wrong — I re**named** the room.
Now every wall in every house echoes my bloom.
They **named** me wrong, so I re**named** the book
Now every word I spell leaves every room shook
I am **not** your **norm** — I am the **natural** tide that rises,
Notorious, nonconforming, nullifying their disguises.
Not made to shrink — I stretch space.
I am the rhythm rebels can't erase.
I **am not** for profit, I am for prophecy.
They monetize the moment — I make memory.
No script written with me in mind, so I pen pages that bend time.

1

No more margins — I manifest middle.
They tried to mute me, I played the fiddle.
They tried to mute me, I turned to cymbals,
loud echoes breaking still rituals.
They tried to mute me, **now** I'm the whistle
in the wind, a subtle call, moving steady through the visuals.
They turned the heat on, **now** I'm the griddle
cooking dreams, flipping pain to brittle.
They can't crack the code, cause I'm the riddle
— deep lines, quiet struggles, prolific, I'm pivotal
Never a phase — I'm the frequency.
Truth in my tone, that's divine decency.
Narrative ninja — shadow-slicer, truth igniter,
Ghost in the system, a silent fighter.

I'm **not** the **noise**, I'm the **note**. Every "no" I flipped into a quote.
Not their **norm** — I am the **nuance** they deflected.
Not their **net** worth — I am the **nectar,** unseen and protected,
Rooted in quiet soil where forgotten dreams are collected.
Named myself in the **noise,**
the system's stepchild, always **neglected.**

Still nested in **nobility**, standing tall, **new name** earns respect,
I mapped out the mess, a cosmic quest,
No GPS — just marks worn like a crest.

I ghostwrite for the gone, script silence in song,
Make memory immortal, where the **nameless** belong.
From **no-name** to **North Star**, I climbed through the fight,
Still stitched by the system, but **now** I am the light.

They **never nurtured** me — I'm self-**named, noble** by **nature.**
Navigating noise like **nebulae** — **naysayers** fade in my favour.
Never not Black, **never not** bold.
Not your **narrative** — I'm the **new** mould.
Needed no nod to **narrate** my truth.
Nubian nomad navigating proof.
Numbness was **normal** — **now** I am the **nerve.**

Not just surviving — I **nourish**, I serve.
No one **noticed** — now I am the **news**.
Not your **neutral** — I am **nuanced** hues.
Named for **nothing** — now I am **known**.
nest in mirrors. I **nourish** my own.

Negativity? I noose it,
learn all their tricks — and then I transmute it.
Narrative necromancer, I conjure truth from the tomb,
Resurrect stories, buried too soon.

I am the **NEW N** word—
natural, necessary, native, nimble, and **noteworthy**

Never your "**no**" — I am the **now**
New North of the **not-yet nation**
Narrating no more **need** for their validation.
New name, new note, new knowing, no fear.
Newness is my **nature** — I am whole, I am clear

I acronymized my struggle, alchemized the pain,
Turned the scars to stars, **now** I'm running my lane.

L-Y-O-N —
a mantra, a mission, a move,
Lift Yourself Over Negativity —

When I show, I prove.

WOULD YOU READ THE BOOK?

Would you read the book if you knew the ending?
If the path was straight, no twists worth tending?
If the lines weren't blurred, broken, or bending,
would they be worth fending and mending?

If the heroine never slipped,
Never cracked or lost her grip—
never fell, never questioned her spell—

Would her triumph still feel transcending?
Would it ring true or feel like pretending?
Where she falls down beginning of ascending

Would you watch the movie if there were no twists?
If fate played fair and fear was dismissed?
No shadows, no wounds, no walk-through flames—
No losses, no lessons to reclaim—
If the rising action never came,
Would you still remember her name?

What makes a story worth telling at all
Isn't perfection—it's the stumble, the fall.
It's the silence that taught her to sing,
It's the break that revealed her wings,
It's the cliffhanger that dared her to crawl.

The main character bends—that's how she grows.
She faces the dark and learns to glow.
The arc is the art, the fall is the gift,
The turn in the road is the power to shift.

So no, I wouldn't read just for the end—
I'd read to see her break and mend.
It's the doubt she faced, the truth she found,
The plot she twisted from the battleground.

The chapter's messy, the margins stained—
Each loss she turned into what she gained.

To walk with her through what tried to destroy her,
And witness her rise, every plot twist employ her—

Because I learned: you are a powerful creator.
The main character, narrator, illustrator.

Reframe your story
Reclaim your glory

Those are words worth reading, the tale worth telling,
The soul that refused, what the system was selling

So if you ask me why I write or why I fight—
Why I show up, share light, take back the night—
It's because I know the beauty in the bends,
The sacred tension before the end.

And remember—

Life will give you lemons.
You decide their limitations.
Will they stay sour?
Or will you taste transformation?
Will they be proof of the pain?
Or juice for your elevation?

If I told you everything, she became
And everything it took
Would you want to find out how

Would you read the book?

START

When you can't decide
Which way to go
You've got to start somewhere
Might as well be here

Start doing
Stop wishing
Stop losing
Start winning
Stop stopping
Yourself when you're at the beginning

Start trusting the process
And holding the vision
Stop adding up your thoughts using division

Start making it make sense
Stop leading on defence/the fence
Stop finding ways to blend
Stop finding ways to dim your light
Start putting up a fight acting like you give a damn
Start appreciating life while you still stand
Start reminding yourself for this food that you prayed
Stop wishing for more and not cleaning your plate

Start going
Start moving
Start showing and proving
Stop knowing, not doing
Start meaning
And being
The change that you're seeking
Stop turning blind eyes from the horrors you're seeing

Stop faking it
Start making it

Start Breaking generations of curses
breakthroughs reverses
The tables are turning
Start being discerning
Stop arguing with fools who are hurting
The pain that they serving
You ain't deserving
Start being you
Stop caring
What the others do
Start using your voice
to shake the room
Starting right now
Stop saying
soon
Start alone
Start together
Start at home
Start whenever
Start smart
Start clever
Start unsure
Stop never
Start scared
Start stupid
Start scarred
Start weird
Start small
Start big
Small steps
Big wins
Start small
Start big
Small steps
Big wins
You got to start
You got to start
You got to start
Somewhere
You got to start

You got to start
You got to start
somewhere
You may not be
Where you want to be
But starting somewhere
Out there
is the key
You got to start somewhere
Might as well be here
When you can't decide
Which way to go
Start somewhere
Might as well be here

ENOUGH (PAULA'S INTERLUDE)

The only thing that's keeping you
From getting you
What you want
Is the story you keep telling you
If you change
Everything you say to you
Everything you say and do
Will change for you

The only thing you can change
When you can't change where you're at
Perspective on what you have
And how you think what's good is bad
When sometimes good is just what's familiar
Comfort to a fool like clouds lined with silver
Sometimes the things you think that are bad
Are really good things you never had
And what is truly valuable
Is how you know which way to go
How you know which do's are don'ts
And how you find the will to won't
Stay within your comfort zone
Be your own detective, inspector of conceptions
That misdirects the senses and critical deceptions
You believe was senseless
But you still accepted
And if you accepted
Then you can reject it

Your mistakes are only a reflection
Of who you were
And they are not directions
To where you're headed
You can still go everywhere you want to go
And nowhere they expected

Your mistakes are only a reflection
Of who you were
And they are not directions
To where you're headed
You can still be everything you want to be
And nothing they expected

For too long
You put their feelings
About you
Before your feelings
About yourself
These feelings
Became thoughts
And they dwelled
These feelings
They got caught
And they swelled
And these feelings
They flow
Right over your wellness
No, you are not well
Yes
You are up the creek without a paddle
No paddle, and you're up the creek
And they herded you from cattle
Cause you acted like a sheep
Someone who is strong
But acts like they are weak
Even when they're wronged
Allowing them to speak
Following along
Pretending to be
Someone who they're not
Someone happy
You put yourself down
To bring others up
You pour into them
Till you emptied your cup

And now you're so thirsty
Deserted by love
Somehow you're still drowning
Don't feel
Like enough

You are more than a dysregulated nervous system rooted in
unhealed trauma
This is how many stay reeling in drama
Thought you was a period
You're really a comma,
The best is yet to come
Should really be your mantra
Things you need to tell yourself
Is what you tell your daughter
Your son, or your sister, or your mother, or your father
This is what I mean when I say
Heal Ancestral Trauma
Scars on the pretty things
Put away the petty things
I'm letting go of anything
That keeps me from discovering
I am more than everything
The world has left to offer

I am enough in the skin I am in
I am enough in the skin I am in
I am enough in the skin I am in

And everything that I want in this life, I can win
I am the master of my mind

The alchemist is I

And I decide
to define
How I live
by my design

I am enough in the skin I am in
I am enough in the skin I am in
I am enough in the skin I am in

And everything I want in this life, I can win

I am the master of my mind

The alchemist is I

And I decide to define how I live by my design

And so
The only thing that's keeping you
From getting you
What you want
Is the story you keep telling you
If you change
Everything you say to you
Everything you say and do
Will change for you

IF YOU CHANGE EVERYTHING THAT YOU SAY TO YOU

I AM ENOUGH

EVERYTHING YOU SAY AND DO, WILL CHANGE FOR YOU

MAKING LEMONADE

I am making lemonade
I am taking bitter situations
And replacing them
With sweet affirmations

I am no longer putting up
With any hesitation
I know I'm good enough
Great is my designation

Learned on the journey
Which is the destination
And the price has gone up
I have some stipulations

I came from a seed

to reclaim my power

I am no longer
begging, pleading
or chasing
Miss me with the
Negging,
demeaning,
and
Wasting
Of my time,
Energy

And so their placement;
in my mental space,
it becomes vacant.
No longer blatant,
disappears
And it erases.

When life looking sour
I do not cower
I came from a seed
To reclaim my power
When they throw me shade
I make Lemonade
out of everything they gave

Pain is my power
fuel that I need,
to keep me in the tower
Queen of the kingdom
Bloom like a flower

Bittersweet
is this proclamation
life will give you lemons
you decide their limitations
And whether or not
This will be a validation
Of how far
you will go
in your imagination
How high you will reach
is within your delegation
Will they stay lemons
Or will you manipulate them
See them as they are
or as they can be created

We are lemons from seeds
With potential
for greatness
Breaking through
rock bottom
Making it out of
dark places
only cause it's sour
that we know
What the sweet taste is.
Taking the good with the bad
Is how we can face it
Doing all that we can
to try to embrace this

Take all the shade
Make lemonade
Out of all the pain they gave
Make Lemonade
Stay in your tower
And do not cower
Queen of the kingdom
Bloom like a flower

Queen of the kingdom

bloom like a flower

14

SATURN'S EPIPHANY

Beef, nah
since I went vegan
I only speak when I got a reason
I know some people
here for a season
They betrayed me
I took that as treason

To sender I return
All of they concerns
No longer govern
Me, I'm from Saturn
Breaking the pattern
Mind over matter
That's how I shatter
All of they words
And they mindless chatter

There was a time
When I would whine
Thinking an eye for an eye
Was the why
Every night I would cry
Look up to the sky
I would say
Take me away
I wanna go
Don't wanna stay
Take me away
I wanna go
Don't wanna stay

Growing up
I had it rough
Not many girls
that looked like me
Said that
I was too much

Then I had an epiphany
Won't let em get to me
They are not equally
Fit to be next to me
New phone who dis
Why is you textin' me
Now you just vexin' me
You better stop testin' me
take you to the streets
like my name is Sesame
You a big bird and
You need to get from me

I'll say this respectfully
demise ain't my destiny
Greatness is meant for me
why I went right
left all negativity

I once heard
don't argue with fools
From a distance
Can't tell who's who
Shame on you
You Shame me one time
Won't be as nice
you shame me twice
No more peace sign
Shame me three times
I must align
With the Divine
Enjoy the ride
Let karma drive

I'm never too much
know that I am enough
my ancestors are
In my blood
Through my veins
Is all they pain
And all my gains
Heal all the shame

I was born to reclaim
Our stolen names

Flying just like Mikey
Doing it, I'm Nike
Goddess of victory
In my blood is they history
My birth is they legacy
The fruit of their labour
They'll never eat

Kandaké's
grand baby
With that god like energy
I'm a queen
So's my team
Tried to squash us like a bug?
We a hive
We've arrived
Can't sweep us
under rugs
We outside
You better hide
time to get you all inside

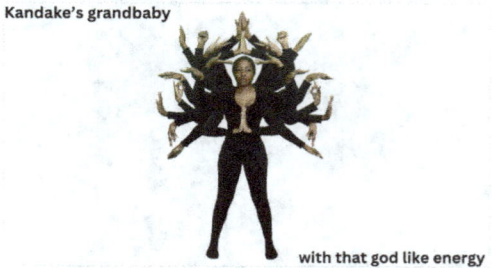

Kandake's grandbaby

with that god like energy

Are you D.U.M.B
Don't Underestimate My Brilliance

My D.N.A is spelled resilience

You tried to finish us
You can't diminish us
Know you wish
you was us

Look at the skin that I'm in
Nubian filled melanin
Meant to shine
when it's bright
And when devoid of light
Filling up their eyes
Take over their minds

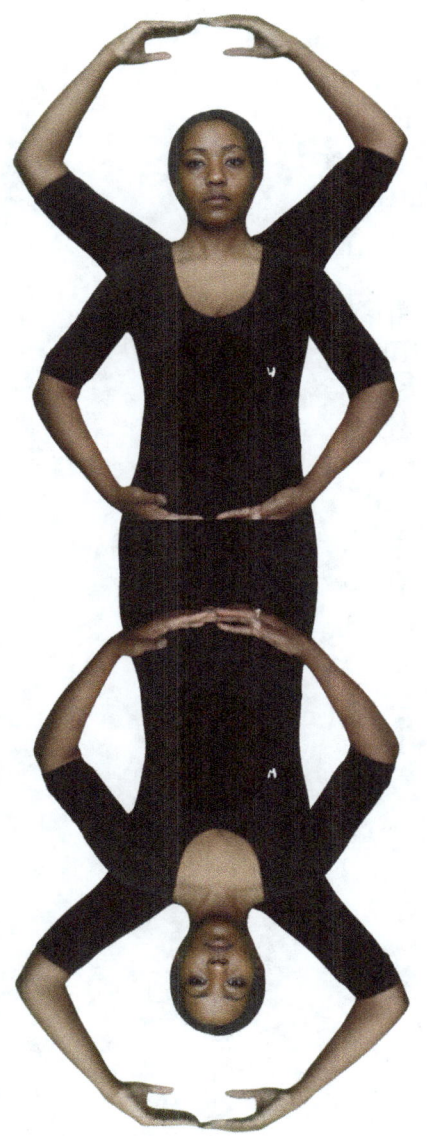

Every wrong I will right
With every song that I write
Skilled sailors
Sail the roughest seas
And as far as I can see
Outstanding in the scene
Got em stanin' out
they green

Just like the grass
We it cut back
We is awake
We see the snakes
Get out the rakes
Weed out the fakes
Do what it takes
Off with they head
I said what I said
Off with they heads
I said what I said
Bad mind fi dead

So to preface
What you'll witness
Is survival of the fittest
Evolution of a flower
Who has come into her power
Finding new ways to empower
Taking everything she learned
Learning new ways to discern

Who is Iron?
Heart of Lion?
Born in Zion?

Took me a while
Energy spent
Finally I made my way
To ascend
I'm breaking the pattern
Send em to Saturn

No I'll
Never dull my spark
Keep shining in the dark

They want me to go
But imma stay
Cause I got out
my own way
I'm breaking the pattern
send em to Saturn

No I'll
Never dull my spark
Keep shining in the dark

They want me to go
But imma stay
Cause I got out
my own way
I'm breaking the pattern
send em to Saturn

STRONGEST OF THE FITTEST

We are the children of the strongest and fittest
We bear the mark of the ones who are gifted
Bred for upliftment
Born from circumstances not decisions
Engrained in our DNA is the blueprint for precision

The ability to rise over oppression
Account ability we count the lessons
From ancestral experience as our blessings
The answer to the colonial testings
continual underinvesting and over arresting
Of our daughters and sons but
We are destined
To prevail over their quest with our questions

Their labels, all fables
Designed to uphold the pedestals and cradles
Glass houses, unstable
no rewinds or reverses
so We cut the cables
The foundation of generations of curses
The revolution will now be televised
through streaming
There will be no rehearsals
The umbilical cord was media —
Fed us illusions through screens
like encyclopedias.

We burned down crosses on the walls
of plantations and churches,
Where they twisted the truth
and repackaged it as worship.

Deceived the ones before us,
made 'em forfeit the seed,
Traded the worth of their children
for a scripture they'd read.

For a false salvation
Across the ocean
To a new world
A new nation
They faced trials
Now we are tribulations
Testimonies of their
battle cries and untold stories
We are the children of their glory

Forgiving all of those who
trespassed against us
Reclaimed our skin
As bronze and not rust
Absolved their sins
Within our wins

And where they stopped

We begin

BENT

Do I deserve it?
Did I put the work in?
Was it all worth it?
gifts and the curses
lines in these verses

I asked myself daily
Was it me
Who failed me
believing the crowd
When they called me crazy
Behave like a clown
Then cry like a baby
Took off my crown
Did nothing to save me
And that's why I blame me
Started to drown in the cream and gravy

So thirsty
But firstly
Let me drown out
All of the ish that came out they mouth
And All of the curses
seem to surmount
To all of the things
I am devout to
Everything
that I can amount to

I'm doubling down on my discipline
I made me a promise
I will invest

Pages unturned
stories untold
You get what you work for
You get what you earn

That's somewhere between deserving and earning
That's somewhere between yearning and learning
The tables are turning
And I am discerning
Which one of these bridges is really worth burning
becoming a person
the very best version
of me is serving
And I am swerving
all of the things
that no longer serve me

I gotta master myself
I got a question
keep on asking myself

What life about?

Curbing my doubts
Put in the work
Before it work out
Knowing your worth
can only amount
To all the thoughts
that you choose to count

They say the past is the greatest teacher
But must be let go to get your future
Keep looking on from the bleachers?
That's like starring in a movie
where there are no features
Then wonder why all your enemies friends
Solid as a rock, concealing the gems

Stay focussed on I
and not on them
not on what I got
but on what I put in

I don't know the day
But I know I will win
The end of one chapter
Is where I begin
Straight as an arrow
Write wrongs with my pen
They thought I was broken
I only was bent

ACTION ALLEVIATES ANXIETY

QUEENIN'

In the name of
Yaa Ashentewaa
Nzingha
Cleopatra
Nepheretti
Durga
Sita
Ganga
Kali

I am healing
I got this feeling
I am revealing
I am healing

All these pains inside my bones
They is leaving
All these doubts inside my mind
That were scheming
I'm intervening on they plans
Got me steaming
But I'm cheesing like I'm glad
And the reason
Why they mad and retreating
Tried to tell me who I am
Don't believe em
I'm a queen in every land
Got a fan in every stand
So they greening
Empress is who I am
Got the Sage in my hand
to do the cleaning

I am healing
I'm revealing
Got this feeling

I'm queenin'
I'm calling all my deities
cleopatra nephretitis
Breaking colonizer treaties
Making ways to feed the needy
Taking anyone who greedy
Underhanded or they seedy
And bury doubting feelings in the ground
Understanding that they freedom won't give out
And there's no eating
with a closed mouth

Nzingha
Angola
Yaa Asantewaa
From Ghana
Kali born from Durga
Sita is my ganga
Ride through on makaras
Chanting out the mantras

Blazing trails
Hotter than a sauna
Only folding into asana
Never in a drama
Transforming trauma
Softer is calmer
Salute to the Sun
I'm a goddess
Very
modest
honest
And demure
Very
mindful
Assertive
And secure

Nzingha
Angola
Yaa Asantewaa
From Ghana

Kali born from Durga
Sita is my ganga
Ride through on makaras
Chanting out the mantras

Hands high, up in a mudra
Yeah she in a mood ya
No one can ever school her
She be the teacher and the tutor
She is the rule and the ruler
The suit and the suitor
The loot and the looter
The past present future
They cute but she cuter
They true but she truer

If they don't choose her
That's how they lose her
No one can ever be her
No one can ever move her

Nzingha
Angola
Yaa Asantewaa
From Ghana
Kali born from Durga
Sita is my ganga
Ride through on makaras
Chanting out the mantras

I called on you
You came for me
Showed me things they didn't want me to see
They didn't want me to know
Because of you I glow
Now I show up
Now I'm bout to hit my blow up

Cause of you I got my dough up
Cause of you I show me more love

Because of you I glow
Now I show up
Now I'm bout to hit my blow up
Cause of you I got my dough up
Cause of you I show me more love

Nzingha
Angola
Yaa Asantewaa
From Ghana
Kali born from Durga
Sita is my ganga
Ride through on makaras
Chanting out the mantras

Orisha Oshun
Queen of the moon
Mother of the water
Birthing sons and daughters
Nobody taught her
The brick and mortar
source and the sorcerer
The light to the torch
Her being is freeing
Giver of the living
Liver she is giving
Everything that's missing

A vision in her mission
Her divination
A goddess
Demure and modest
God body model
Protector of deceptions
And any weapons
Now her blessings
She is sure

never guessing
She the answer
to the question
Applies the knowledge
to the lesson
Her Confessions
She confesses
She is blessed
And she is destined

MY HEROES

I want to tell you
about my heroes
The ones who taught me about winning
Whose passion and hard work
Are truly, what's giving
They made being great
A professional living
They took a stand
They paved the path
So I don't trip
They got rid of the branch
With me in spirit
Guiding the way
I say
Asé
Asé
Asé

My heroes are people
Who Set trends and the pace
passing on the batons
They've run their race
But Life's a marathon
So it's time to take their place

My heroes are
Visionaries with a mission
Like Nipsey Hussle,
His lyrics, blueprints for ambition
Hustle, motivate, chin the sky
Rise above challenge and
aim for new heights

My heroes
Are people
Who make hard decisions
I wanna be like Kobe
24 on the clock he was mister consistent
Shooting his shot with laser precision
My heroes are people who define definition

My heroes
Are people who
Inspire nations
People like Virgil
Abloh using fashion
as communication
A social tool for change
And a path to elevation

My heroes
Are those
Who Seek reparations
through our liberation
By any means necessary
Malcolm X taught me dedication
And that the future belongs to
Those who take great preparation
To get what they see in their visualizations
My heros are dreams that became manifestations

My heroes are alchemists
Making something from nothing
Maya Angelou phenomenal woman
Who's life taught me one thing
life can give you lemons
So it's up to you to make it sweet
Take sour situations and reframe what it means

My heroes are people
Mans like Bob Marley
Who turned pain into power
And into melodies

My heroes are people like
Dr. Sebi
Who taught me
My health is my wealth
And food, vitality

My heroes are people
Who lived mindfully
My heroes are people like
Mohammed Ali, a boxer, a father
and a man of peace,
Who preached as he walked and walked as he preached
Float like a butterfly,
Sting like a bee,
Cause The hands can't hit what the eyes can't see.

My heroes are lessons I've learned to believe
My heroes are reflections of who I can be
My life is a testament to their legacy
My heroes are blessings that live out through me

CLIMBING MOUNTAINS

Overcame obstacles
Overcame opposition
The ops is opportunity
Blinded by their vision
And others opinions
Their wants and their wishes
Guide your inhibitions
Mistrusted intuition
Attention paid
Is how division
Strays
becoming our existence

For a time we caved
Underneath their rage
We had no say
Yet we found a way
to shine to glisten
Ancestors made
It's out the ditches
They left us messages
we listened

Stop asking for permission
Take back our hieroglyphics
Our rest is
our resistance
The trails we blazed
Define resilience
We standing on business
This poem is the witness
The master of our decisions
Only washing our own dishes
So when you see her in the kitchen
Let her cook
She just enrichin'
Do the most
With what she given

Haters will say
that she just coastin'
But she knows her privilege
So she ghost em'

Never liked beef
She won't roast em
She wants peace
So she toast em
While she drinking
and the whole time
She be thinking
Grateful that she didn't
Stay down
And stayed living
For it was when she was drowning
that she learned
to just keep swimming

These micro aggressions
The sum of her depression
The only way through is
The opposite
Artistic expression

Displays
of how the distance
Made
her complicit to
Oppressive impositions
Kept her
missing
the mission
Trading
Economical decisions
Swaying
political positions
Knowing we are all human
But we don't live the same conditions

She took the pen as her sword
And slayed her demons
stayed the course
Trusting the process
And redeemed it
So Her-story was rewritten
On the Eve
of the day
The apple was bitten
Becoming the author of her story
His-story
undergoing adamant revisions

They say behind every good man
Is a greater woman
I am inclined
To believe
I am a spirit being human
arose like a rose
And my soul has finally risen

Treat others how I want to be treated
And not how they treat me
Meet them where they're at
But don't match their energy
Kill all of them with kindness
Colour and gender bias
Might be my business
But I don't mind it
Cause I am on to
bigger mountains
that I am climbing
My timing is set
I am aligning
With no regrets
I'm deciding
What I manifest
Is divine

And showing up at my best
Is my vibe
Say it with my chest
Turbulent are the tides

When I lost
Their waves
Of thoughts
And the people pleasing
And the fan girling stopped
And I remembered that I call the shots
And the only way you can sell out is if you let yourself
get bought
After everything that I've been taught,
And how hard those before me fought
for my freedom
I will not get lost
In the holes of colonial story plots
I engage with the page
I connect the dots
then I hit the stage
and I done the talks

And if what I say
leave them in shock
Make him move and shake
So their brains don't rot
Then I pray they find a way
To say go
When they want to stop
And use those barriers as building blocks
Find your way out the hard place
between the rock
Leave your troubles at bay
by the dock
Before your time runs out on the clock

The very definition of brave
It's to feel the fear and do it anyway
Some people say that they want change
but don't want to change their ways
of thinking
So they are doomed to stay the same
glass half full while their ship is sinking
The water under the bridge
Becoming their master
Surfing in a tsunami
A natural disaster
It never slows down
You just get faster

Life is a series of varying chapters
Life goes on past happily ever after
So how you read it
will be a reflection of how you see it
You can really have it all
If you choose to believe it
And just maybe
Let em do it
When they call you crazy
It's often a sign
Of being right
too early
You may not win now
But you will win surely

When they sleep on you
You got to tuck em in
Your come up
Is vindication
going for it all
going for the glory
The underdog
On top
Only ending to my story

✦ SPELLWORK ✦

NOW THAT YOU HAVE READ MY SPELLS, IT'S YOUR TURN TO CREATE YOUR OWN.

In spellwork, transmutation is the magical process of transforming energy or circumstances from one state into another, usually turning something negative or limiting into something positive and empowering. It's about taking what no longer serves you—fears, doubts, pain, obstacles—and changing them into strength, clarity, confidence, and success.

Think of it as alchemy for the spirit: turning lead into gold, shadows into light, struggles into spells of power. Transmutation spells help you release old patterns and create new, uplifting realities through intention, focus, and the power of words or ritual.

Now It's Your Turn

On the next few pages, you will write your own spell of transmutation.

I've included prompts to guide you through the process, but feel free to let your words flow freely—no rules, no limits. This is your sacred space to explore your past, focus on your present, and envision the future you want to create.

Remember, your words are powerful— they are your spells.

SPELLWORK: TRANSMUTATION PRACTICE

——————— ✦ ———————

Explore your past. Engage your present.
Elevate your future. Empower your life.

Create a personalized I AM affirmation that transforms
emotion into action and doubt into direction.

Step 1: Explore Your Past
Reflect: Think about a challenging moment in your
past that shaped you.

What did you overcome?

Write a few words or a short sentence:

What inner quality helped you get through it?

□ **Resilience** □ **Courage** □ **Patience** □ **Hope**
□ **Inner Strength** □ **Self-Belief** □ **Faith** □
Determination
□ **Other:** _____

This becomes your Root Strength →

————————————————————————

Spell Space: Write any lingering thoughts and/or emotions
that you are experiencing in this moment, before moving on
to the next step

REFRAME YOUR STORY
RECLAIM YOUR GLORY

SPELLWORK:
TRANSMUTATION PRACTICE

————— ✦ —————

Explore your past. Engage your present.
Elevate your future. Empower your life.

**Create a personalized I AM affirmation that transforms
emotion into action and doubt into direction.**

Step 2: Engage Your Present

What emotion are you feeling most right now?

□ Fear □ Doubt □ Overwhelm □ Anger □ Insecurity
□ Sadness
□ Other: _____

What is this emotion teaching you or asking you to notice?

□ Awareness □ Boundaries □ Trust □ Self-worth
□ Stillness □ Discernment
□ Other: _____

This becomes your:

Present Emotion → _____
Lesson Keyword → _____

Spell Space: Write any lingering thoughts and/or emotions
that you are experiencing in this moment on the next page,
before moving on to the next step

REFRAME YOUR STORY
RECLAIM YOUR GLORY

_____

_____

_____

_____

_____

_____

_____

_____

_____

_____

_____

_____

_____

_____

_____

_____

_____

_____

_____

_____

_____

_____

_____

_____

SPELLWORK: TRANSMUTATION PRACTICE

———— +.+ ————

Explore your past. Engage your present.
Elevate your future. Empower your life.

Create a personalized I AM affirmation that transforms
emotion into action and doubt into direction.

Step 3: Elevate Your Future

Who are you becoming? Who is your future self?

□ **Grounded**   □ **Radiant**   □ **Free**   □ **Creative**
□ **Brave**   □ **Aligned**   □ **Unapologetic**   □ **Compassionate**
□ **Other:** _____

This becomes your

Future Vision → _____

Spell Space: Write any lingering thoughts and/or emotions
that you are experiencing in this moment on the next page,
before moving on to the next step.

REFRAME YOUR STORY
RECLAIM YOUR GLORY

_____
_____
_____
_____
_____
_____
_____
_____
_____
_____
_____
_____
_____
_____
_____
_____
_____
_____
_____
_____
_____
_____
_____
_____

SPELLWORK: TRANSMUTATION PRACTICE

———— +.+ ————

Explore your past. Engage your present.
Elevate your future. Empower your life.

Create a personalized I AM affirmation that transforms
emotion into action and doubt into direction.

Step 4: Empower Your Life

What action, intention, or quality do you want to activate
today?

☐ Speak ☐ Build ☐ Rest ☐ Ask
☐ Create ☐ Lead ☐ Trust ☐ Heal
☐ Other: _____

This becomes your Empowered Action →

_____

Spell Space: Write any lingering thoughts and/or emotions
that you are experiencing in this moment on the next page,
before moving on to the next step.

REFRAME YOUR STORY
RECLAIM YOUR GLORY

SPELLWORK:
TRANSMUTATION PRACTICE

———————— ✦ ————————

Explore your past. Engage your present.
Elevate your future. Empower your life.

**Create a personalized I AM affirmation that transforms
emotion into action and doubt into direction.**

Step 5: Claim Your Identity

Complete the sentence: I am...

☐ **Worthy**   ☐ **Enough**   ☐ **Ready**   ☐ **Whole**
☐ **Chosen**   ☐ **Divine**   ☐ **Limitless**
☐ **Other:** _____

This becomes your Final Identity →

_____

Spell Space: Write any lingering thoughts and/or emotions
that you are experiencing in this moment on the next page,
before moving on to the next step

REFRAME YOUR STORY
RECLAIM YOUR GLORY

SPELLWORK:
TRANSMUTATION PRACTICE

———————— ✦ ————————

Explore your past. Engage your present.
Elevate your future. Empower your life.

Create a personalized I AM affirmation that transforms
emotion into action and doubt into direction.

Your Personalized Affirmation

Fill in the blanks using your answers:

I am (Root Strength) _____
rising through (Present Emotion) _____
into (Future Vision) _____
I transmute (Present Emotion) _____
into (Empowered Action) _____
I am (Final Identity) _____

Example:

I am courageous, rising through uncertainty into bravery.

I transmute uncertainty into mindful action.

I am magical.

Note: Feel free to rearrange the words and play with the tenses before completing your spell to make it make sense to you.

Spell Space: Write any lingering thoughts and/or emotions that you are experiencing in this moment on the next page, before moving on to the next step

REFRAME YOUR STORY
RECLAIM YOUR GLORY

Final Reflection & Invitation

You've journeyed through spells of courage, strength, and transformation — and now it's time to bring your own magic to life.

Remember: your story is powerful. Your words are spells. Every time you write, you craft your reality and shape the life you want.

COMING SOON: DELUXE EDITION

In addition to these beautifully crafted spellbooks, a deluxe
collector's edition of the full L.Y.O.N. series will be released in the
future—offering a richer, more immersive experience with:

All spells from every volume compiled in one place
Expanded activities and interactive journaling prompts
Immersive spells that come alive through audio formats (Songs,
voice notes, Soundscapes) and visual elements that deepen
engagement and connection

**EXPERIENCE THE ELEVATION
@ THE DIGITAL DEN de LYON**

**Learn more on my website:
www.iamelledelyon.com/lyonspellbook**

For now, these spellbooks serve as your essential companions,
grounding you in each step of the journey towards self mastery as
you build toward the complete collection.

WHAT'S NEXT?

This is just the beginning.

The next book in the series will dive deeper into spells of
empowerment and elevation — tools to help you keep lifting
yourself over negativity and into your fullest, most radiant
self.

Stay connected, stay inspired, and keep casting your spells.
Your next chapter is waiting to be written!

THE DEN DE LYON

Your journey doesn't have to be solitary.
Share your spells of courage and transmutation

**Snap a photo of your writing and tag @elledelyon @pdaglobal
on social media using the hashtag #LYONBOOK**

By sharing, you might be featured and even have your
work included in upcoming books in this series.

**IF YOU WANT TO GO FAST, GO ALONE
IF YOU WANT TO GO FAR, GO TOGETHER
- African proverb**

STAY ELEVATED

We are just getting started!

If you feel called to co-create, collaborate, or connect— for creative projects, sacred tools, or clarity on your next step-- reach out.

Let's elevate your mindset, empower your life, and bring your vision to light.

Instagram/Tik Tok/Youtube/Linkedin: @elledelyon

Creative Consulting: @PDAGlobal

For Bookings & Inquiries: info@iamelledelyon.com

Keep rising, keep roaring,
Sow seeds and keep soaring.

REFRAME YOUR STORY
RECLAIM YOUR GLORY

You are already winning—
this isn't the end
it's just beginning.

See you in a spell!

www.ingramcontent.com/pod-product-compliance
Lightning Source LLC
Chambersburg PA
CBHW081006120626
46546CB00010B/3029